Blind Faith & Ivory Tusks

Johnny Erickson

Presentation by *BookLeaf Publishing*

Web: www.bookleafpub.com

E-mail: info@bookleafpub.com

ISBN: 9789357445528

First edition 2021

PREFACE

maybe it was legit...

Blind

I reached out to touch something
what it was I didn't really understand
I just hoped it was something viable
something real
as I patted around the surface
tried to comprehend it in my mind
what could constitute the touch sensations that i
faced
i wondered if any of it was real
or if it even really mattered
if any of it was true substantial
but i'm just blind
feeling around
lost in the dark
hoping to catch a spark
literally
just to feel some warmth
to feel not so taken advantage of
to just feel

First dance

The heart split iron
the rapture of blood from a ventricle
pushed through and expelled
Breath heavy
a sprinter spent with a couple miles left
the clock running empty
but this was finally it
the now or never
shake off the in-between
the anxiety filled with fear
the left behind
the buzzing in ear
the changes of a new season
what will become of the B.C.
as we cross over to a new plane
A.D.
It's all about the let down
the lack of magic
the misunderstood meaning
the life lacking a proper ending
the storybooks filled with lies
were is the value in heartbreak
where is the value in your eyes
the dead stare that greets me
in every reflection found

not in this moment
not on this night
not now

The Nervous Embrace

Count down to an assertion
a cataclysmic way of ruining lives
with a quick glance
heavy breathing and tight feelings
it's all in her jeans
above them two bars with bearings
from the milky white
she's undone
slowing unraveling the pieces of me
the pieces I keep too close
stuck in the hull of a hollowed out chest
when I close my eyes
her's still stare out
wondering if it is something she has done
it's not for a lack of caring
it's the totality that is creeping in
keeping cautious for every interaction
the unprepared still reeling
but for yet one last bitter embrace
to embark one final time
through the lost strands of knowing
what forth we had left behind

Convenience Store

There is cold comfort
that comes with the convenience
of knowing what will absolutely happen
but you know that it is usually a lie
like the phrase "Things will be fine"
or perhaps the one that goes
"I bet this will be the best night"
It's a let down sealed with a kiss
a conflicting contraction of loose lips
that flutter over teeth
a clattering calamity when the sets meet
what's worse is when you know
it's far too cold to walk home
but it's too late to call anyone to give you a lift
maybe an old flame
to put behind a centuries of worries
behind a pharmaceutical reset
but don't worry
"It's all gonna be fine"

Card Tricks

The bones protruded outwards
piercing out further than my feelings of shame
when you told me you didn't care at all
and invited me to stay
here I was to think of some code of honor
that could be ever so simply undone
like the clasp that unclasped so quickly
behind your back from a simple pinch of an
index and thumb
An anxious look of worry downplayed
I drowned it out by bottles of booze
all to be left teetering for balance
a connected concocted escape route
that only got me closer to the destination
you spent the majority of the time talking of
your frustrations
about another guy
and if he would ever leave her for you
I stayed quiet
not necessarily sure what to do
cause I didn't want to lie to you
but wasn't sure I could spare you the hard truth
that it wasn't happening
he wasn't ever going to leave her for you

Her Ears

She stood silent
in a warm embrace
looking up with a longing
a desire in her eyes
a love in her heart
a hope for one truth
as she held me ever so tightly
her hand grasped my neck
as I placed my lips upon her cheek
my eyes closed tight
she then kissed me deeply
in the cold hours well past midnight
her earlobes so tiny so quaint
I kissed them softly
as she then let out a sound of relief
She gripped me much tighter
before releasing but yet grabbing my hand
leading me with her
she explained,
"don't make too much noise"
She led me thru the snaking hallways
up to her hotel room,
when we arrived it was a frenzy
her clothing was shed
as I placed her upon the bed

I grasped her legs tightly
my head buried in her thighs
kissing the soft petals of a flower
fresh from the rain
I engorged in her beauty
in a space where time is forgot
the holy promise land of a perfect love
that has been found right under your thumb
and I really did love her
as much as I would try to convince
myself other,
for after all these years
I still think of her
and the soft kisses I placed upon her delicate
ears

Those Eyes

I'll always remember those eyes
and the look that entailed them
that fire that blaze
it wasn't even a spark or a sparkle,
but an inferno.
you were ready to burn,
to fill me full of your desire
yes, you burned ever so bright
you were a picturesque painting
pontificated with a beret
perched upon your crown
we shared drinks in a two bit bar
that might as well been a strip club
dim lit but illuminated by those eyes
ever shining
ever fixated on me
we stumbled out at bar close
the busses stopped
you called for a cab to take me home
and I truly didn't know
that that it would be your own
for the evening
in the morning we'd awake
naked and stretched out
in a heat challenging the January sun

your fire always burning
till it burned me alive

Divinity

I see you in bloom
like a rosebud
your body quivers when it needs some
your hands shake
The back breaks
breath
you need some
but you keep asking for a light choke
I'm broke
and then some
but I'm not done
so don't come undone
not just yet
I don't mean to be mean, but then again
I am and ever am I
I oblige with a squeeze
and then some
sometimes when my eyes fall on you
i can not construe the ways
in which you move
Mesmerized
your body breaks the prism
the spectral shifts
your eyes
they scream fire and wine

as I continue to dine
on the overwhelming plater
placed before me
your body
mmmm
the true divine

Diving

Faceless yet loved
I am into all of the parts of you
that are surface level
I stand afar to gaze out
at a mountain landscape
I think to myself how beautiful
the country can be
and when I see you
I think how beautiful God can be
to bless the world with such grace
I am but just a boat floating in your sea
I've never truly dived in
to that which lies beneath
to the true nature of your magnificence
to the beauty of your spirit and soul
that which you have kept safe within
but I want to be vulnerable
I want you to swallow me whole

The Tease

I'd tease you
kiss your collarbones clean
kiss your neck
to behind your ears
I'd let you feel the warmth of my breath
as I move my mouth to your temples
sliding my hand from your knee up to your
thigh,
I'd kiss the corner of your eyes,
and cup your pussy just to feel the heat that has
come alive
tracing a line with my finger up,
I'd kiss your forehead
to the tip of your nose
move my hand over your waist to your hips
your ass
and squeeze as i trace your lips with my own
kissing the corners till i finally meet the middle,
with one hand a fist full hair,
my other your ass,
tilting your head back
to taste your lips

Jesus Mornings

We once were wolves
running high on a night sky
through blanketed forests filled with freedom
excitement clasped our hearts
almost as much as love did
you looked at me and howled
I looked at you and admired
when did you loose it all so
you simply lost control
you said you didn't feel pretty
and that's why no one would ever love you
you didn't even realize that I loved you
you slept over my parent's house
you said you felt safe
as you climbed into my bed
and I was afraid to get close to you
but I managed to get just close enough
to catch the warmth from you
the warmth from your beauty
the same beauty you didn't think you had

Film Booth

She looked at me
with eyes soft and brown
she was faint like a fawn
majestic like the sea
with a magnetism
that guided me six states away
I watched her hips sway
as she struggled to carry
the weight of our twenties
and the creation of my ideal love story
sitting knee to knee
as the flash bulb flicked away
capturing the awkwardness
of a boys jaw dropping
while he developed feelings
one strip of four frames
eyes still endearing
tucked away in a box of belongs
left alone with lost feelings

Just Like The Movies

I walked with you down the beech
sand beneath my feet
it was like a dream
and I came to you
the meet cute I always ever wanted
to be able to tell
patchouli and pine needles
is what you called me
I was going through a gin phase￼
you were diet coke and rum
and a wholesomeness I wasn't used to
as I was smoking cigarettes
asking you not to tell my loved ones
we looked around and noticed we were forgotten
following unknown paths back
we paused to look out at the sea beyond us
I never been in this ocean
so you pulled me in
and in an embrace that I always imagined
I kissed you
before drunkenly stumbling
pushing you in

the waves came by softly
the salt water entangled your hair
you said you needed to shower
then asked "aren't you coming in?"

See You Around

I'm a mess
was left alone for far too long
wound up getting drunk again
I call you for a ride
you say once again
this will be the last time
as you put on your coat to come to my rescue
if I had any sense I'd keep drinking
try to end this night
cause when you get here
I'm still sober enough to remember my regrets
like ever calling you in the first place
and for kissing you in that bar
and for telling you I love you
when I really wished I loved myself
you help me into the car
as I'm unbuttoning my coat
in a few minutes time
we'll find ourselves immersed
in each other
a common trend
I swear to God I'd drown in your eyes
but the hurt won't come until the morning
sunrise
when I pick up my coat

and say see you next time

Car Crash Love

I stand back
bracc for impact
I always knew your love
would wind up a car crash
you gave every bit of yourself
to someone who never valued themself
and that's why I never understood
how you could fall in love so fast
maybe there's more understanding
in a car crash
in fact I think I understood that most of all
the chaos that I created
with all of my lines and lies
when I replied "I love you too"
those were more palpable
than ever grasping your love
and I'm not saying you came on too strong
No, I'm not saying that I never felt love
It's just that I never knew how to love myself
and in that
how could I ever love you

Shout

You see
the things that you don't understand
the things you didn't get
I wanted to give
I was ready
but the longer I knew you
was the more I knew
that it couldn't be you
I never conned you
I wanted the same things
and even after I started having doubts
I still wanted to believe
that maybe
maybe it could still work out
you say we have nothing in common
you say I never give my opinions
and it's all so true
because we really do
have nothing in common
nor share similar views
you said that I'm afraid of you
and that that is my fault
that you didn't cause that
as you yelled again

The Window

Maybe it's May
the month you wanted to be bold
and we have the conversations
and it's still never told
what could have been
or still could be
between us
as you tell me about your new beau
the object of your affections
and I'm affected by wondering
all the times you said little things
and the ways you glanced at me
if in any of those moments
that maybe you wanted me
but if the window is closing
do I let it shut once again
do I finally own up
try getting back in
cause the main thing holding me back
that keeps me a ship at bay
is that I already told you I loved you
and you said "no you don't, don't say that"
and let me walk away

Forlorn

You got me forlorn right now
cause I just keep thinking of all
the memories we could have
but we won't
and maybe that's okay
life can't be without pain
and you can hope for connection
but you can't guarantee
there is no knowing that it would be romantic
there is no knowing if it would be serene

The Rosary

I put my trust
my faith
I put my hope
in a love
but as time moved on
the rosary shown
the love was anything but
it was a vengeful god
a jealous and angry obsession
the prideful seeking praise
the lepers seeking reprieve
I prayed for forgiveness
was rewarded with petulance
pay penance
a Hail Mary nailed to my head
a crown of thorns crafted into cuffs
cutting off the circulation
I began to breathe heavy
and yet I yearned for communion
to take the body
the flesh onto thee
to drink from the holy cup
to be forgiven in your name
I cut out my eyes
because they could see,

faith is far more romantic
when love is the dream

Literally

I hate you
that's what you said
and you expected me not to believe that
that I'm in the wrong for thinking it's done
for taking things too literal
when literal wasn't what you had exclaimed
you said silence is when it's over
as I fumble for words
fumble for thoughts
fumble through emotions
not knowing where to stop
wondering why all of this is happening
what was my fault
where did I fuck it up
and how can I fix the torn pieces
that keep pulling apart
and now we've moved on
but only in name
for the feelings are never forgotten
and the forgiveness is only in vain
you said you always remember
and now when it's subtly brought up
from time to time
I play silence
my greatest claim to fame

still not being able to tell you
that I didn't know how you worked
that yeah, I took things so literal
till I literally fell apart

Memories

I kept every single one of your letters
I never had the heart to throw them away
like the way you threw me out
They sit in a box in the back of my closet
just gathering dust
like you sit in the back of my brain
I only think of you ever so little so often
littler and littler each year
when the small things that trigger your presence
fade more and more
and the memories of you
are now just your home
the few choice moments that I tried to leave
alone
to keep untouched from the parts of you that I
hated
the parts of you that polluted my feelings
I keep these small memories as trinkets
I shine them up and polish them
I no longer look at them with love
but a lust for what was
and I only look at them when I'm truly lonely
when I think back at the times where you
thought you were so alone
and I kept trying to reach out and wave my arms

trying to explain to you that I would be your
home
but you didnt open your eyes
and I never spoke
and we stood there never sharing true emotions
till it broke
and I don't blame you for how things went down
I mostly blame myself
but much like these memories even that
is fading now
and you're just somebody
I'd rather not talk about